Reading Success Mini-Books

SHORT & LONG VOWELS

Twenty Interactive Mini-Books That Help Every Child Get a Great Start in Reading

by Mary Beth Spann

SCHOLASTIC
PROFESSIONAL BOOKS

New York ● Toronto ● London ● Auckland ● Sydney ● Mexico City ● New Delhi ● Hong Kong

Cover design by Jaime Lucero

Interior design by Ellen Matlach Hassell
for Boultinghouse & Boultinghouse, Inc.

Illustrations by Ruth Linstromberg

ISBN: 0-439-08677-9

Contents

Introduction

Welcome to *Reading Success Mini-Books: Short & Long Vowels*. This book provides a fun and easy way for young children to experience short and long vowel letters and sounds. Beginning readers will really benefit from completing and collecting all 20 of these little books. When used as a regular part of a balanced approach to literacy—one that includes reading, writing, speaking, and listening—these mini-books will provide children with an easy-to-understand, concrete foundation for short and long vowel sound/symbol mastery.

Research tells us that children learn vowel letters and sounds best when they're presented in a meaningful context. Each short and long vowel mini-book introduces children to a group of simple, illustrated words that feature the same vowel letter sound. Each mini-book offers children the chance to practice writing and reading these words, and provides a simple review activity so children can test themselves on what they've learned.

The books' small size means they are a breeze for young students to complete, store, collect, and keep. They help give children a sense of mastery and ownership over the vowel sounds they are learning. In a way, these mini-books serve as children's own print-awareness progress reports. As children successfully work through the books, it's easy for them to see how each one represents an important step on the road to reading.

Assembling the Mini-Books

1. Make a double-sided copy of the mini-book pages.

2. Cut the page in half along the solid line.

3. Place pages 4/5 on top of pages 2/7 as shown.

4. Fold the pages in half along the dotted line.

5. Check to be sure that the pages are in the proper order and then staple them together along the book's spine.

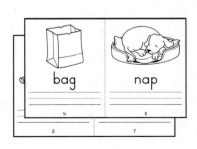

How to Use This Book

This book contains 20 mini-books, one for each short and two for each long vowel sound in the English alphabet. There are also five books that present words featuring long and short variations of each of the five vowels. How you introduce and share these books with children will largely depend on how you introduce vowel sounds in general. But no matter how you choose to use them, you'll find these books to be small but powerful page-turners. Here are some ideas for putting them to work in your classroom:

Pre-assemble Mini-Books as Needed

Instead of asking children to assemble these books in class, you may want to assemble a complete class set ahead of time. This prep-step allows students to focus their attention on the mini-books' content, rather than on construction. Remember: Parents who are unable to volunteer in the classroom may welcome this task as something they can work on at home.

Let the Books Serve You

Here are some quick tips for making the mini-books a successful part of your reading routine:

- If you introduce short and long vowel sounds to the whole class in a particular sequence, you might introduce the mini-books in that same sequence. Each student, or small groups of students, may then work on the same vowel-sound mini-book simultaneously.

- For a more individualized approach, in which each child learns letters and sounds at his or her own rate, you may make the books available to children on an "as needed" basis. Perhaps you can display an alphabet border at children's eye level, with a supply of mini-books stored in envelopes pinned beneath each vowel letter, or set up a vowel-learning center stocked with the mini-books. When individualizing, keep a mini-book checklist showing which ones each child has completed. Be certain to schedule student/teacher conferences so you can assess and celebrate children's progress.

- As children learn how to read and spell the words in the books, consider transferring the words to word wall lists. Invite children to write and illustrate additional words for each list. Encourage children to refer to their mini-books and/or word walls when writing stories and books of their own.

Introducing the Mini-Books in Class

1. Show children how a book is constructed and what they are expected to do on each page.

2. Work through one mini-book together.

   a. Read the cover together. Demonstrate how to use the "Name" line. Call attention to the configuration of the letters printed there.

   b. Call attention to the picture and word on each page. When children correctly identify a picture by reading the word, invite them to explain their reading strategies. In doing so, you are asking children to pay attention to the print features of the word below the picture.

   c. Demonstrate how to copy the word on the line provided. Suggest to children that if they think they already know how to spell the word, they can try and cover the word below the picture and write the word without peeking.

   d. Show how the back-cover activity serves as a self-checking review page. (Tip: The back cover can also serve as a screening page. If you suspect a child already knows how to read, spell, and write all the words in the mini-book, you can ask him or her to complete this page before completing the whole book. That way you'll know if the child needs to move on to a mini-book that is at a more appropriate instructional level.)

Mini-Book Extensions

- Meet periodically with each student to review mini-books together. To organize their mini-book collections, give each child a large metal loose-leaf ring. Punch a hole in the upper left-hand corner of each completed mini-book and slip each one onto the ring. Store collections in a multi-pocketed shoe bag (hanging on a wall or from a doorknob), or hung on wall hooks.

- A tree trunk and branches decorated with a few paper leaves makes a nice bulletin-board backdrop for displaying new books (before adding them to the rings). Just tack individual books to the branches so they resemble leaves. Title your display "Leaf Through a Mini-Book!"

- Set aside class time for children to take turns sharing one book of their choice.

- Designate one day a week as "Mini-Book Take-Home Day" so children can share their growing library with family members.

- Provide blank mini-books so children can write and illustrate their own vowel collections with a theme (for example, *Animal Words with Short A*).

- Call attention to short and long vowels in the words that surround you. Notice the vowels and vowel sounds that help spell street signs, labels, book titles, and characters' names. Call attention to unusual or unexpected spellings featured in vowel variants. Notice how the addition of one vowel (for example, *mat/mate*) can change a word's sound and meaning.

Generating Family Support

1. When familiarizing families with instructional materials and strategies you plan on using to teach reading and writing, introduce phonics mini-books as part of your overall approach.

2. Emphasize that a well-balanced program includes phonics plus many other strategies for reading, speaking, listening, and writing with children. Share specific examples of how you include these components in your program.

3. Invite families to extend learning at home by reading aloud together every day, by calling attention to any written materials that fills their days, and by reviewing schoolwork—including mini-books—with their children.

Name each picture.
Color those with Short **a**.

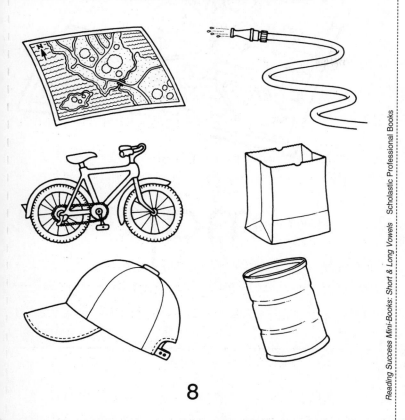

8

Name _____

Reading Success Mini-Books: Short & Long Vowels   Scholastic Professional Books

1

can

6

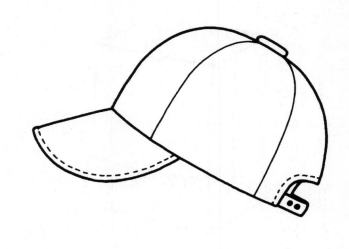

cap

3

bat

2

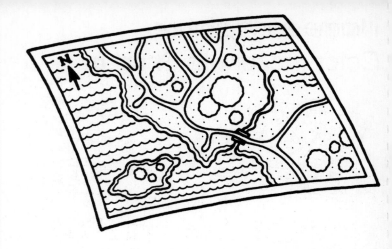

map

7

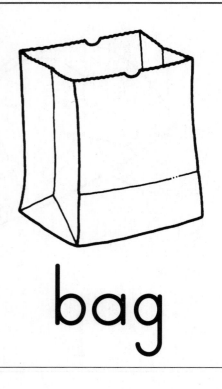

bag

4

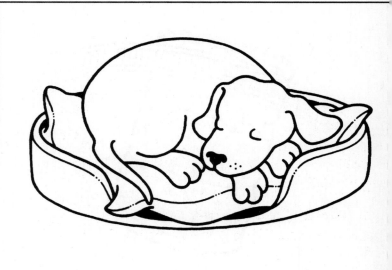

nap

5

Name each picture.
Color those with Short **e**.

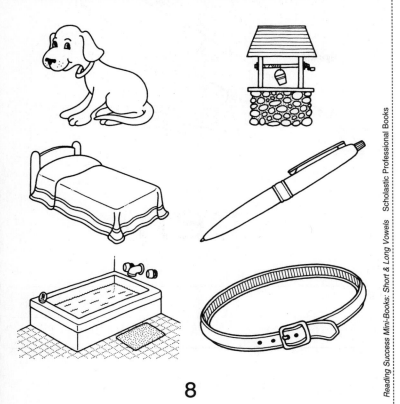

8

My Book of Words
with Short **e**

_____

Name _____

1

Reading Success Mini-Books: Short & Long Vowels   Scholastic Professional Books

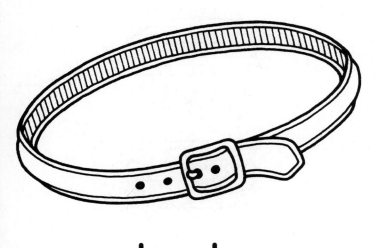

belt

_____

_____

6

leg

_____

_____

3

bed

2

pen

7

bell

4

well

5

Name each picture.
Color those with Short i.

8

Reading Success Mini-Books: Short & Long Vowels   Scholastic Professional Books

My Book of Words
with Short **i**

Name _____

I

fish

_____
_____

6

pig

_____
_____

3

bib

2

six

7

king

4

chip

5

Name each picture.
Color those with Short **o**.

8

My Book of Words
with Short **O**

Reading Success Mini-Books: Short & Long Vowels   Scholastic Professional Books

Name _____

1

mop

6

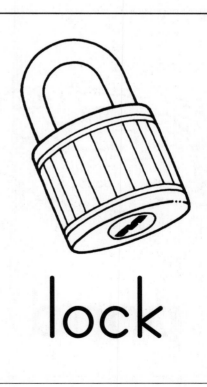

lock

3

box

- - - - - - - - - - - - - -

2

fox

- - - - - - - - - - - - - -

7

pond

- - - - - - - - - - - - - -

4

block

- - - - - - - - - - - - - -

5

Name each picture.
Color those with Short **u**.

8

My Book of Words
with Short **U**

Reading Success Mini-Books: Short & Long Vowels   Scholastic Professional Books

Name _____

1

truck

_____

6

mug

_____

3

duck

_____

_____

2

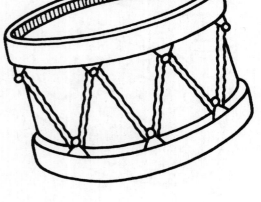

drum

_____

_____

4

bug

_____

_____

7

pup

_____

_____

5

Name each picture.
Color those with Long **a**.

8

My Book of Words
with Long **a**

Name _____

1

rake

_____

6

flakes

_____

3

gate

2

skate

4

cave

7

cake

5

Name each picture.
Color those with Long **e**.

8

Reading Success Mini-Books: Short & Long Vowels   Scholastic Professional Books

Name _____

I

queen

6

steam

3

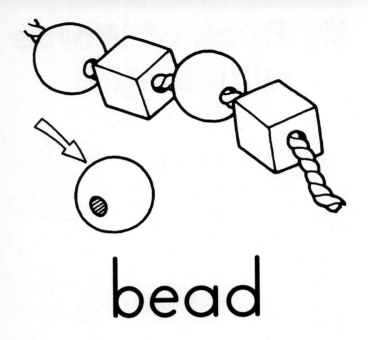

bead

_____
- - - - - - - - - - - - -
_____

2

jeep

_____
- - - - - - - - - - - - -
_____

7

beach

_____
- - - - - - - - - - - - -
_____

4

wheel

_____
- - - - - - - - - - - - -
_____

5

Name each picture.
Color those with Long **i**.

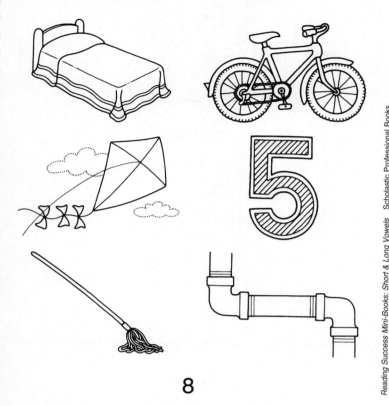

8

My Book of Words
with Long **i**

Name _____

1

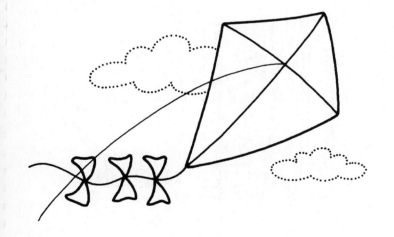

kite

6

mice

3

bike

2

five

7

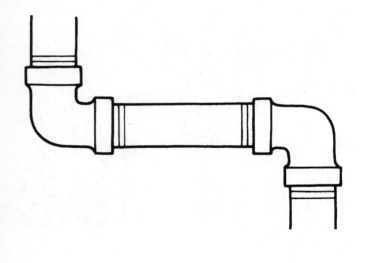

pipe

4

rice

5

Name each picture.
Color those with Long **o**.

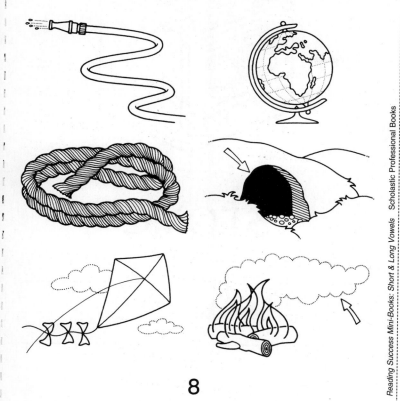

8

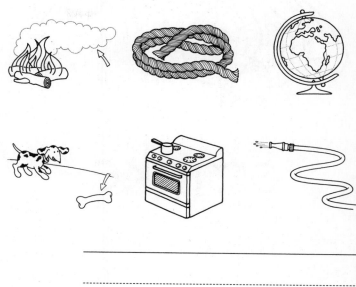

Name _____

I

Reading Success Mini-Books: Short & Long Vowels   Scholastic Professional Books

globe

_____

6

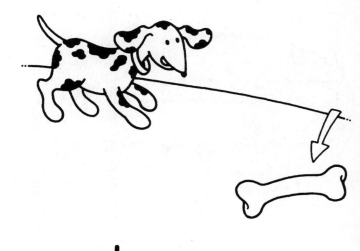

bone

_____

3

smoke

_____
- - - - - - - -
_____

2

stove

_____
- - - - - - - -
_____

7

rope

_____
- - - - - - - -
_____

4

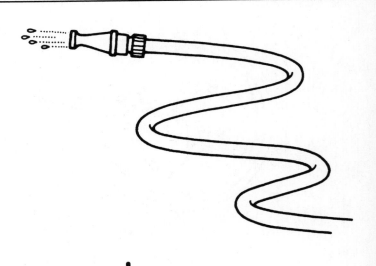

hose

_____
- - - - - - - -
_____

5

Name each picture.
Color those with Long **u**.

8

My Book of Words with Long U

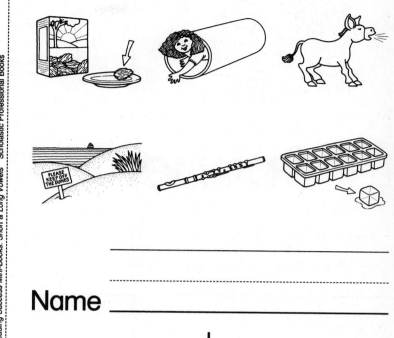

Reading Success Mini-Books: Short & Long Vowels   Scholastic Professional Books

Name _____

1

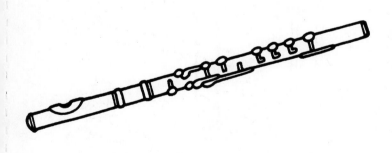

flute

6

mule

3

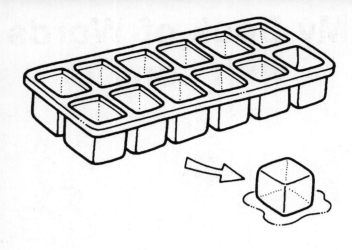

cube

_____

- - - - - - - - - - - -

_____

2

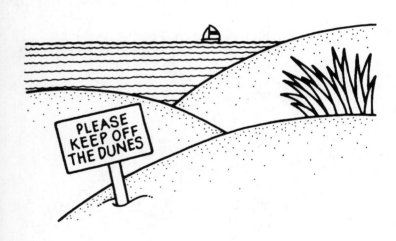

dune

_____

- - - - - - - - - - - -

_____

4

PLEASE
KEEP OFF
THE DUNES

tube

_____

- - - - - - - - - - - -

_____

7

prune

_____

- - - - - - - - - - - -

_____

5

Name each picture.
Color those with Short **a**.
Circle those with Long **a**.

8

My **Book of Words**
with Short **a**
and Long **a**

_____

Name _____

Reading Success Mini-Books: Short & Long Vowels   Scholastic Professional Books

1

man

_____

6

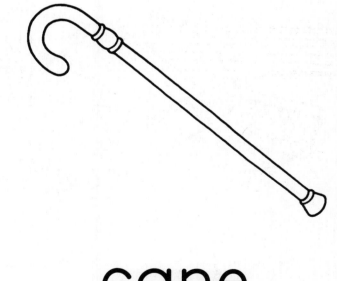

cane

_____

3

can

mane

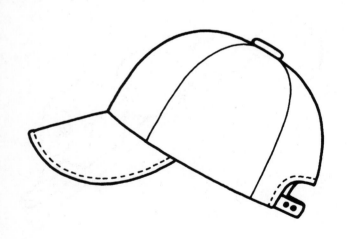

cap

cape

Name each picture.
Color those with Short **e**.
Circle those with Long **e**.

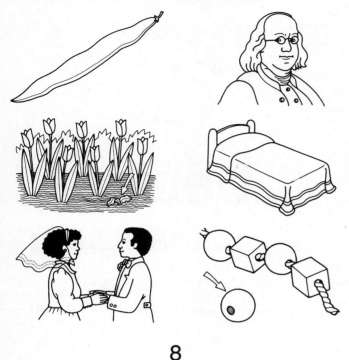

8

My Book of Words
with Short **e**
and Long **e**

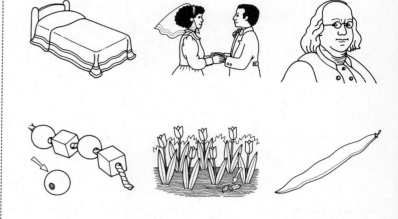

Reading Success Mini-Books: Short & Long Vowels Scholastic Professional Books

_____
- - - - - - - - - -
Name _____

I

Ben

_____
- - - - - - - - - -
_____

6

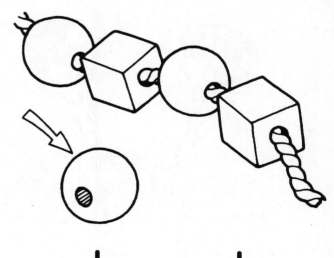

bead

_____
- - - - - - - - - -
_____

3

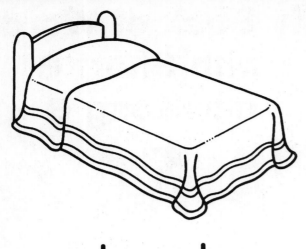

bed

2

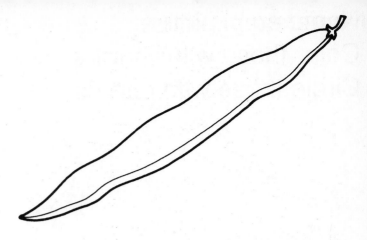

bean

7

wed

4

weed

5

Name each picture.
Color those with Short **i**.
Circle those with Long **i**.

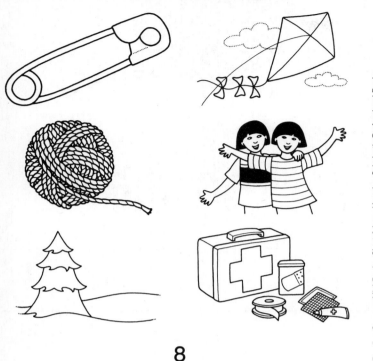

8

My Book of Words
with Short **i** and Long **i**

Reading Success Mini-Books: Short & Long Vowels   Scholastic Professional Books

Name _____

1

twin

6

kite

3

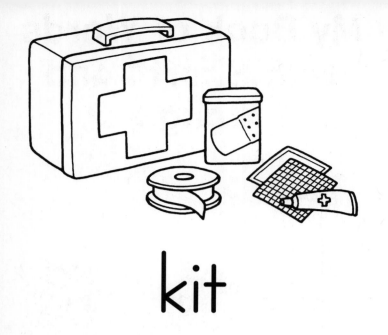

kit

_____

2

twine

_____

7

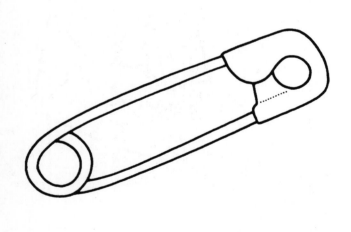

pin

_____

4

pine

_____

5

Name each picture.
Color those with Short **o**.
Circle those with Long **o**.

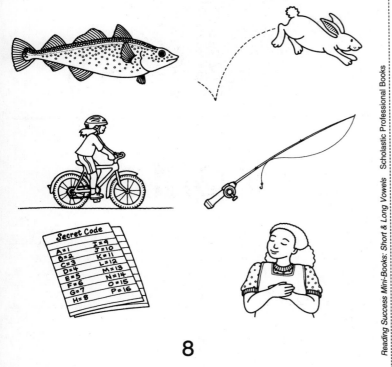

8

Reading Success Mini-Books: Short & Long Vowels   Scholastic Professional Books

My Book of Words
with Short **O**
and Long **O**

Name _____

1

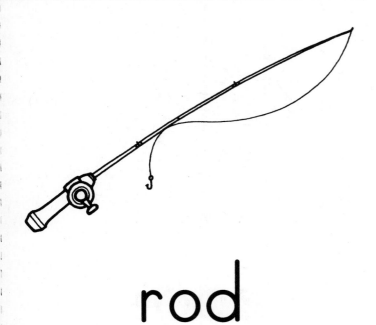

rod

6

hope

3

hop

2

rode

7

cod

4

Secret Code

A = 1	I = 9
B = 2	K = 11
C = 3	L = 12
D = 4	M = 13
E = 5	N = 14
F = 6	O = 15
G = 7	P = 16
H = 8	

J = 10

code

5

Name each picture.
Color those with Short **u**.
Circle those with Long **u**.

8

Reading Success Mini-Books: Short & Long Vowels   Scholastic Professional Books

My Book of Words
with Short **U**
and Long **U**

Name _____

_____

I

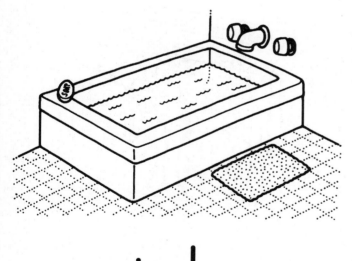

tub

_____

6

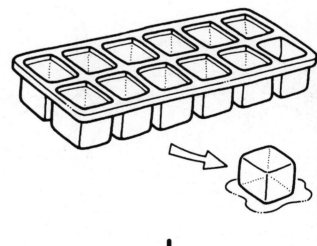

cube

_____

3

cub

2

tube

7

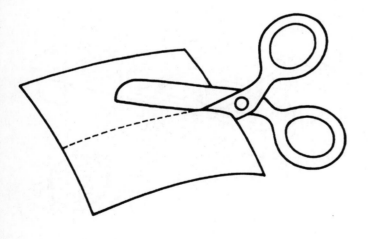

cut

4

cute

5

Name each picture.
Color those with Long **a**.

8

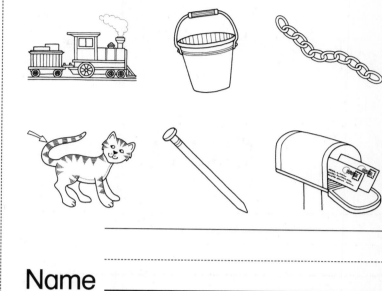

Reading Success Mini-Books: Short & Long Vowels   Scholastic Professional Books

Name _____

I

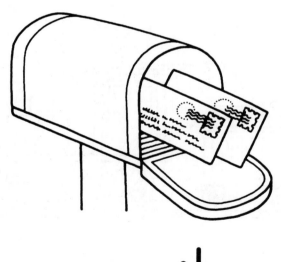

mail

6

chain

3

pail

- - - - - - - - - - - -

2

nail

- - - - - - - - - - - -

4

tail

- - - - - - - - - - - -

7

train

- - - - - - - - - - - -

5

Name each picture.
Color those with Long **e**.

8

My Second Book of Words with Long **e**

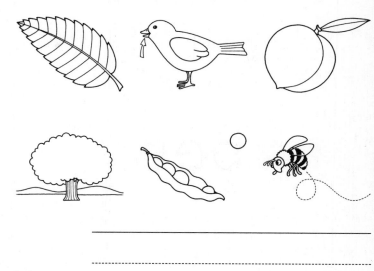

Name _____

1

Reading Success Mini-Books: Short & Long Vowels   Scholastic Professional Books

peach

_____

6

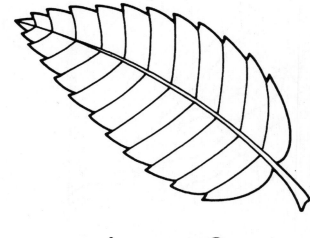

leaf

_____

3

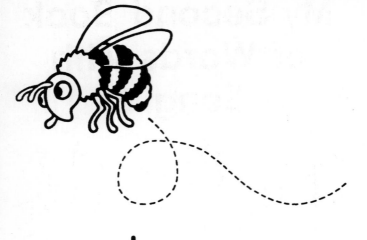

bee

2

beak

7

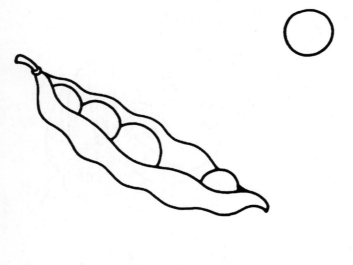

pea

4

tree

5

Name each picture.
Color those with Long **i**.

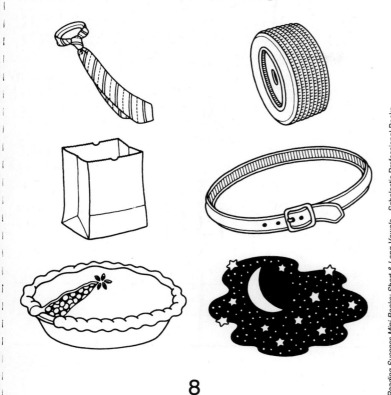

8

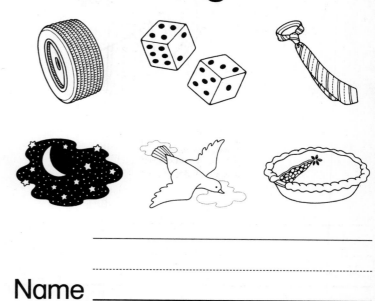

Reading Success Mini-Books: Short & Long Vowels   Scholastic Professional Books

Name _____

1

pie

_____
- - - - - - - - - - - - - - - -
_____

6

dice

_____
- - - - - - - - - - - - - - - -
_____

3

tie

2

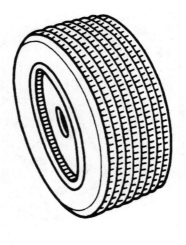

tire

4

fly

7

night

5

Name each picture.
Color those with Long **o**.

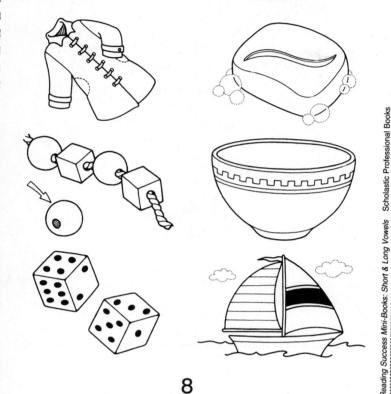

8

Reading Success Mini-Books: Short & Long Vowels   Scholastic Professional Books

My Second Book of Words with Long O

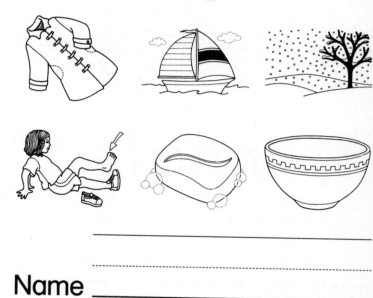

Name _____

1

snow

_____

6

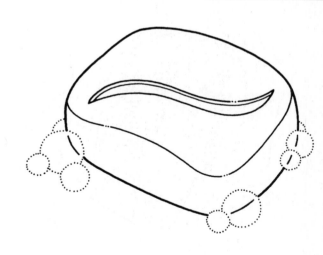

soap

_____

3

boat

_____

2

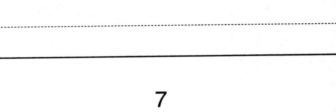

toe

_____

7

coat

_____

4

bowl

_____

5

Name each picture.
Color those with Long **u**.

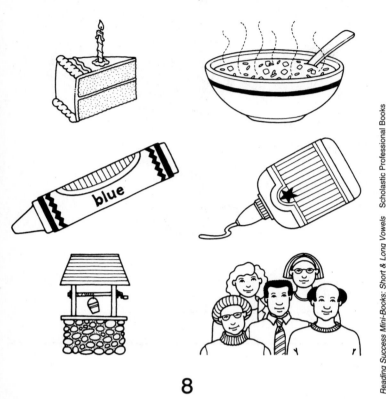

8

Name _____

1

Reading Success Mini-Books: Short & Long Vowels   Scholastic Professional Books

group

_____

6

spruce

_____

3

soup

2

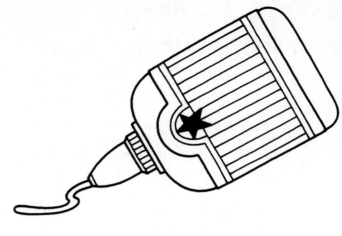

glue

7

June

4

blue

5